Neighbors

Chiara Lubich

Neighbors

Short Reflections on Loving the People Around Us

Compiled and with a Foreword
by
Bill Hartnett

New City Press
of the Focolare
Hyde Park, New York

Published in the United States by New City Press
202 Comforter Blvd., Hyde Park, NY 12538
www.newcitypress.com
©2012 New City Press of the Focolare

Cover design by Leandro de Leon

A catalog record is available from the Library of Congress.

ISBN: 978-1-56548-476-4

Printed in the United States of America

Contents

Foreword

This book deals with a central reality in Chiara Lubich's spirituality of communion: the neighbor. Indeed, "the neighbor" is a lens through which all of that spirituality can be examined. It includes love of neighbor as well as eleven other "points": God-Love, the will of God, the Word of God, the new commandment, Eucharist, the gift of unity, Jesus crucified and forsaken, Mary, the Church-communion, the Holy Spirit and Jesus present in our midst. Chiara often referred to these "twelve points" that emerged from the experience she and her early companions shared during World War II in the devastated city of Trent. She said that these points are interconnected in a Trinitarian way; each stands on its own, but also contains all the others. Living one means living them all. And some of them are not merely points or topics. Some, as Chiara reminds us, are God's very self; one of them is the Mother of God. Unique to this spirituality of communion is the constant presence of others, of neighbors with whom we are to be drawn into unity (see Jn 17:21).

When Chiara was learning to live this new communitarian form of life, her Teacher began by revealing his immense love for each person. "God loves you immensely" was his first lesson. Chiara felt an immediate urge to share this discovery with her neighbors, her first companions. Together, they were able to say, "God loves us immensely" and "We have believed in love" (1 Jn 4:16). Next the Lord showed Chiara how she could respond to his being Love for her: by doing his will. And where could they discover that will? In the Holy Scriptures. There they learned that doing God's will meant living the Words of Life that seemed to leap off the pages and come to life in them (see Mt 7:21; 1 Jn 2-3). Here again, they lived the Words of Life together with neighbors. The Word of Life gathered people together into a new Christian community that later grew into the Focolare Movement.

Chiara was once asked when, exactly, the Lord showed her the centrality of the neighbor in spiritual life. Her simple and honest answer was that she didn't recall a precise moment, but it was probably when they read these words in Matthew's Gospel: "Truly I tell you, just as you did it to one of the least of these, you did it to me" (Mt 25:40). This is what Jesus will say to each person at the Final Judgment.

After reading these words, Chiara and her companions realized that the neighbor was not merely a means or an instrument for loving Jesus. In fact, Jesus addresses these words to people who know that they have loved their neighbors, but do not realize they have loved him. Full of surprise, they ask: "When did we see you, Lord?" Chiara and those other young women in Trent first responded to this question by loving their neighbors, the real people around them, especially the poor and the needy, and soon after—everyone. Theirs wasn't a platonic, detached sentiment of goodwill, but concrete and personal love for real people that involved effort, action and heart. In the spirituality of unity the relationship with God is not a twosome, but what Chiara terms a "trinity": "me, my neighbor, God." The neighbor is not an obstacle between me and God, but a sacred "archway" through whom I come into God's presence, and through whom God draws near to me.

When our love becomes mutual, then "the new commandment, the pearl of the Gospel" brings Jesus among us (see Jn 15:12; Mt 18:20). And Jesus among us makes us one in him. Now my neighbor is not only an archway but, together with me, a complete edifice, "a living temple to the Most Holy Trinity" on earth. Chiara calls this living temple of neighbors made one by Jesus the "Exterior Castle." This expression reveals the profound and sanctifying unity that Chiara saw taking place between brothers and sisters who live with Jesus among them (Mt 18:20). Teresa of

Avila calls the individual soul of an upright person who seeks holiness within an "Interior Castle." At the center of Teresa's interior castle lives Jesus the Spouse and King. In Chiara's exterior castle, Jesus lives and reigns among brothers and sisters united in his name through the practice of his own love, his new commandment (Jn 15:12). The Eucharist makes them into the Body of Christ. The life within this exterior castle is Jesus, the Life (Jn 14:6; 11-25), a participation in the divine life of the Trinity, and the relation between the members is the "Holy Spirit, just as in the Holy Trinity" (see Acts 4:31). As the Fire of Love, the Holy Spirit "purifies and refines" our love for neighbor, and our neighbor becomes both our "purgatory" and our "heaven on this earth." Far from being an obstacle to union with God, our neighbors are a living reminder of Jesus' words: "Strive first for the kingdom of God" (Mt 6:33) and "The kingdom of God is among you" (Lk 17:21).

Love of neighbor also led Chiara to understand more deeply the role that Mary received at the foot of the cross. There, she heard her Son cry out his abandonment by the Father (Mt 27:45-46), and yet place himself again in the Father's hands (Lk 23:46). In that moment Jesus redeemed us, joining himself to us completely (2 Cor 5:21). In that moment, Chiara sees him as the grain of wheat that falls into the darkness of the earth and dies, producing "much fruit," "many new sons and daughters of God." Hearing him say "Woman, here is your son" (Jn 19:26-27), Mary experienced her own abandonment. By "losing" her own Son she shared in his abandonment and found him now— her Son and her God—in many other sons and daughters, the members of his Mystical Body. She became the Mother of all, Mother of Jesus in each and every person. Of that moment Chiara writes: "The Father, Jesus, Mary, us. The Father abandoned Jesus and Mary for us. Jesus accepted the abandonment of the Father and abandoned his Mother for us. Mary accepted the abandonment of the Father (sharing in that of her Son) and of the Son for us. And so we have been given first place. Love does this madness! And so we, for love of our neighbor, should leave Father, Son and Mother when the will of God requires it. The neighbor is our Heaven here on earth." Therefore, Chiara invites us to be like our Mother, to be her heart and her hands for all our brothers and sisters, her children. Mary is the teacher of love of neighbor. When the Word became flesh in her, her first act was to "set out …in haste" to visit and help her cousin (Lk 1:35-45). Chiara invites us to show the same industriousness, the same haste and concreteness as did our Mother, "through our loving service to them" bringing Jesus to others.

Chiara encouragingly reminds us that our neighbor is our great "opportunity" because we pass from death to life by loving our neighbors (see 1 Jn 3:14).

Bill Hartnett

Short Reflections on Loving the People Around Us

Your neighbor
is the person next to you
in the present moment.[1]

~

In the work
of reaching out
to our separated brothers and sisters
we should always
keep Mary before us
as our only model.
And we should develop
those qualities that are so often
associated with her:
patience,
perseverance,
poverty,
spiritual detachment from our riches,
also spiritual ones,
silence,
purity
—all stemming from our love
for our sister, our brother.[2]

"Truly I tell you,
in so far as you did it for one of the least of
these, you did it for me" (Mt 25:40).
Thank you, my God,
for having opened for us
on earth a way,
the straightest
and the shortest way
for reaching Heaven
quickly and directly.[3]

~

Jesus says:
"Truly I tell you,
in so far as you did it
for one of the least of these,
 you did it for me" (Mt 25:40).
These words made our old idea
of our neighbor
collapse completely.[4]

We can't go to God alone,
but we must go to him
with our brothers and sisters,
since he is the Father
of us all.[5]

~

"Be perfect
as your heavenly Father
is perfect" (Mt 5:28).
And when we are perfect as the Father,
we are another Jesus,
another Son of Man.
And this is wonderful
because it means being
a true man,
a true woman.[6]

It's through our neighbor
   that we continually pass
   from an empty and meaningless life
   to a full life: "We have passed out of death
   and into life, because we love our brothers
   and sisters" (1 Jn 13:14).[7]

   ∼

At first,
   the Holy Spirit
   focused our attention
   on the people around us,
   on the least:
   the poor,
   the sick,
   the wounded,
   the imprisoned,
   the homeless,
   the elderly,
   the children ... [8]

When we love our neighbor,
we notice that our union with God
grows.[9]

~

We tried
to solve the problems
of our poor neighbors
through works of charity,
which became the seeds
of social projects
that would later be born.[10]

~

The greatness
of all human beings
lies in the fact
that God has died
for each one of them.[11]

With our neighbor
we can pattern our lives
on the life of the Trinity;
we can erect a temple of God
in the midst of the world.[12]

~

With our neighbor
we can experience
a foretaste of heaven
in this life.[13]

~

Christian humanism is fine
but I prefer to think
that Jesus,
God,
has died for me,
for you,
for everyone.[14]

We still should have
a preference
for the least.[15]

~

When the Christian community begins
with the poor
and the least,
then it's beginning its life
in good soil.
And this foretells
growth,
fruitfulness,
vocations.[16]

~

Lord,
you taught me to love you
in my brothers and sisters,
in my neighbors.[17]

What's most needed
is that we transform
all our relationships
—with brothers, sisters, parents,
relatives, friends, acquaintances,
with everyone—
into Christian relationships,
relationships of love.[18]

～

People who are all tied up
with their personal duties
and seeing the will of God
only in them,
are actually quite attached to themselves.
They're boring, gloomy,
and they often frighten people away.[19]

We do not use
  extraordinary means
  of mortification,
  because in loving our neighbor
  and making ourselves one with them
  —which requires the silence or
  death of our own ego—
  we demolish the old self in us
  and allow our new self to live.[20]

~

Look for and discover
  your own light
  in your neighbors:
  your true self,
  which is Jesus,
  the true you
  —in them.[21]

When you have encountered Jesus
in your neighbor
unite with him there.
Then you and your neighbor
will be a cell, a living cell
of the Mystical Body of Christ,
a hearth for God
with his Fire,
his Warmth
and his Light,
to be shared
with others.[22]

~

It's not enough
to despise evil.
We must radiate goodness,
sincere goodness,
love.[23]

When unity becomes deepest
between us
it distinguishes us
as *new persons*,
Jesus in us,
the maximum affirmation
of the divine and human
personality of each one of us.[24]

~

We are able to have
a true dialogue
when we model ourselves
on the life of the Holy Trinity
where the divine Persons
are eternally One
in a dialogue,
a communion
of Love.[25]

On each person I meet
   Jesus comes to me: as a gift,
   an enrichment, an encouragement,
   a purification;
   and in each person, Jesus wants
   to be loved and served.[26]

~

The *gift* that Jesus gave to us,
   the one mentioned to the Samaritan woman,
   is not human in nature (see Jn 4:3-42).
   Now it is possible
   to share in our neighbor's sorrows
   and worries and joys,
   because the life
   that overflows within us
   is love,
   which is of a divine nature.[27]

Christians cannot help
   having love in their hearts
   for all people.
   It's their nature
   as sons and daughters of God.
   They possess love,
   the very love
   Jesus shares
   with the Father.[28]

~

I felt
   that I was created as a gift
   for whoever was next to me
   and that whoever was next to me
   was created by God
   in gift to me.
   Just as in the Trinity,
   where the Father is all for the Son
   and the Son is all for the Father.[29]

The feeling of being one
   with humanity,
   past, present and future,
   this love for others,
   is the powerful force
   that makes us fit
   for building today,
   and planning a better life
   for tomorrow.[30]

~

"Let us make humankind
   in our image, according to our likeness"
   (Gen 1:26).
   If humanity wants to be
   as God wants it to be,
   it must be in the image of God
   who is Unity and Trinity.
   Human beings should love one another
   as do the Persons of the Trinity.[31]

Only God
   can form His image
   in someone.
   We can only ruin him.[32]

~

Everything can become a way
   to show our love to God
   and to our neighbor.[33]

~

In today's sick world
   Christians ought to spread light
   and the darkness will retreat;
   they ought to spread love.
   This would be the best medicine
   for human perversion to go away.[34]

We must love God in our neighbor
—God distinct from our neighbor—
but God
in our neighbor.[35]

~

"Love your neighbor as yourself."
This is a constant effort
since our nature loves itself.[36]

~

The sun cannot but warm
and love would not but renew,
rejuvenate and bring growth
to every member and group
of the Mystical Body of Christ,
the Church.[37]

*O*ur Lady
didn't go to Elizabeth
to sing the *Magnificat*,
but only to help her cousin.
And so
we should never go to our neighbors
to unveil the Christian treasure
we carry in our hearts,
but only to carry our neighbor's burdens,
to share their joys
—to love them.[38]

*O*ur Lady
isn't a Christian in word only.
No, she travelled some distance
to do a single act of love
for her cousin Elizabeth,
one of those acts of mercy
to which we are all called.[39]

When someone loves
in the present moment,
God lives in him or her.
Then they are guided by the Holy Spirit
and so they don't judge,
or think evil.
They love their neighbor as themselves
and have strength for the
madness of the Gospel:
offering the other cheek,
going the second mile,
and so on ...[40]

~

Every neighbor
whose soul is enriched by grace
is truly another Christ.
Or else a potential Christ,
if that grace is not there.[41]

Jesus has remained on earth
in his priests
through whom,
as Priest and Victim,
mysteriously and divinely,
he continues to offer himself
to the Father
for the whole of humanity;
and similarly,
Mary has remained on earth
in the persons of consecrated virgins
who continue her maternal mission
of service to the members
of humanity,
and of collaboration
in the act of sacrifice.[42]

We can't imagine Mary staring at herself.
Mary looks to Jesus
and, in this way,
finds that she resembles him.
The more we look to our neighbors,
to the Church,
and place ourselves at their service,
the more we are Mary.[43]

~

Whenever we cast the seed
of the Word into the soul
of a brother or a sister,
if it falls on good ground
it is received by the soil.
Then others live the Word
and the Life is in them.
They become Jesus.
And we become mothers
of Jesus in them.[44]

Our Mother, Our Lady Desolate,
   lost everything for God …
   Of course, your gifts and talents
   are meant to be trafficked
   in the sunshine of charity and love
   that must envelope
   all that you do.
   And then you should be forgetful of them,
   lose them,
   so that you can
   be love
   for every brother, every sister,
   for that neighbor beside you.
   Love is only mindful of the beloved,
   —like Mary.[45]

   ~

We try to love those around us
   even in the most insignificant
   circumstances of life.[46]

Our Lady went to her cousin
   to offer help.
She visited her cousin
   only to love Elizabeth.
Then Elizabeth was filled
   with the Holy Spirit
and understood the great prodigy
   that was being accomplished
   in her relative.
And Mary could tell her own wondrous
experience.[47]

~

He is in the depths
   of every soul that is alive to grace.
And if a soul is dead
   because of sin,
then it's a tabernacle
   waiting for God
who alone can give it
   joy and expression
   and meaning.[48]

Seeing and loving Jesus
in a neighbor
means seeing and loving God
in that neighbor.[49]

≈

After God,
with God,
and for God,
our neighbor
holds first place
in our lives.[50]

≈

In each neighbor
may we see a person
in the process of becoming
another Christ.[51]

Be at the loving service
of every person you meet
so that Jesus may be born
and grow
in them.[52]

~

In everyone
see Jesus
who is born,
grows
and lives by doing good
—a new son of God—
who must die
and rise
and be glorified.[53]

~

Your soul
should not be at peace until
through loving service to your neighbors—
you are able to discern
the spiritual countenance
of Jesus in them.[54]

The Father, Jesus, Mary, us ...
The Father allowed Jesus
to feel abandoned by him *for us*.
Jesus accepted the abandonment of the Father
and deprived himself of his Mother *for us*.
Mary shared in Jesus' abandonment
and accepted the deprivation of her Son *for us*.

We have been put first.
Love does this madness!
And so, whenever the will of God requires it,
we should also leave
the Father, Jesus, and Mary
for *our neighbor*.

Our neighbor is our heaven
here below.[55]

Since we are subject to time,
we love our neighbors
one at a time,
without clinging
to any lingering affection
for the neighbor we loved
a moment earlier.
Besides,
isn't it the same Jesus we love
in everyone?[56]

~

All our relationships in life
are actually
with one Person only,
with him, Jesus.
There's actually never anyone
between us and him.
Because when I'm loving a neighbor,
I'm already standing
exactly as I will stand
at the moment of my death:
me and Jesus.[57]

We extended our love
to all.
And there were no longer
limits on our love (see 1 Cor 13:8).[58]

~

We didn't love
because of personal likes
or self-interests,
but because Jesus
had commanded it.[59]

~

At first
we gathered the poor
because we noticed that Jesus
had a special preference for them.
Then we saw that many were poor
of other things.
Even the rich are sometimes
poorer than paupers,
when their hearts are poor
without much love.[60]

*J*esus
somehow makes himself present
in every human being.
In everyone we meet,
we meet the Lord.[61]

~

*F*rom neighbor to neighbor,
all around the world.
From neighbors of every calling
to neighbors of all ages,
neighbors of every social background.
And a great network was spread
across the earth.
Neighbor by neighbor,
we shared each other's joys and sorrows,
—which made Jesus grow in each one of us—
all for one and one for all.
Neighbor to neighbor
until *all are one*.[62]

$\mathcal{L}$et us love
   those who usually
   come into our consideration
   because they are physically
   close to us.[63]

~

$\mathcal{J}$esus took a child
   and put him by his side,
   and said to them: "Whoever
   receives this child in my name,
   receives him who sent me;
   for whoever is least among you is great"
   (Lk 9:46-48).

Jesus overturns everything.
The least are in reality the greatest
and the most important,
because Jesus has put himself on their side.
In fact, whoever receives one of these little
ones
receives Jesus himself.[64]

$\mathcal{L}$et us love
   those who sometimes escape our attention:
   those of whom we speak
   or hear others speak.[65]

~

$\mathcal{L}$et us love
   those whom we sometimes don't notice:
   those for whom we pray
   or those whom we come to know
   on the news, in the newspaper, or on TV.[66]

~

$\mathcal{L}$et us love
   those who sometimes
   escape our notice:
   those who write to us
   or to whom we write,
   those for whom
   we do our daily work.[67]

$\mathcal{L}$et us love
  the living
  and those who are no longer
  here on earth.[68]

~

$\mathcal{L}$et us love
  our neighbors
  both individually
  and collectively.[69]

~

$\mathcal{T}$he most impoverished and unfortunate
  are not the people who die of hunger,
  but the people who after this life
  will never know the life of Heaven,
  because they have rejected God.
  And we have this high calling
  in our Movement
  to devote ourselves most especially
  to these.[70]

$\mathcal{L}$et us love and highly respect
  all the peoples of the earth.[71]

~

$\mathcal{W}$ith her second *fiat*
  on Calvary Hill
  Mary seems to hand over to God
  her divine maternity toward Jesus.
  But it was only in this way
  that she became Mother of every person.
  And here you see our greatness:
  We are destined to be "another Jesus."
  He himself had said: "If the grain of wheat
  does not die, it remains alone. But if it dies
  it bears much fruit" (see Jn 12:24).

If the grain of wheat does not die,
  it remains alone.
  But if it dies it multiplies.
  If the Son of God died,
  it was to give life
  to many sons and daughters of God.[72]

$\mathcal{M}$ary also paid for us.
  And in return for sacrificing
  her Jesus
  may she not receive
  many half-Jesus in return.
  But only other-Jesuses
  with his same light,
  his same love:
  like him.[73]

$\mathcal{O}$nce we have decided for God
  as the Ideal of our life,
  we immediately feel urged
  to put this choice into practice
  by reaching out to those around us,
  sharing their sorrows and joys:
  like Mary who set out with haste
  to visit her cousin Elizabeth.[74]

But the ones
who pull most at our hearts
are that crowd of atheists
from both the West and the East.
These are the poorest of the poor,
for they are poor of God
and possibly the eternal Life.[75]

~

We must certainly love
Jesus Forsaken
in everyone,
but especially
in those who most resemble him,
in those who seem far from God.[76]

~

Each neighbor
is like the archway
through which we must pass
in order to reach God.[77]

We should also love Jesus Forsaken
in the little ones,
the children and youths
who today are being exposed
to a global atmosphere of indifference
practical atheism, immorality,
and much worse ...[78]

What appears so beautiful and new
about the Gospel
is the love that Jesus
invites us to have
for our enemies
near and far.[79]

We are to turn the other cheek,
to go the extra mile
as the Gospel teaches.
And so we have tried to do
whenever some enemy
has crossed our path.[80]

We do what Jesus wants
when we transform our life
into a continual act
of mercy (see Mt 9:13).[81]

~

"Whomever wants to be first among you
must be the very last, and the servant of all"
(Mark 9:35)

Unity with our neighbor
is reached through humility,
by constantly aspiring
to the first place,
by constantly placing ourselves
as much as we can
at the service of our neighbor.[82]

~

Whenever we forget
to love our neighbor,
we begin again,
with that complete concern
for the other's needs
which is the best antidote
for egoism.[83]

Whatever our station in life,
be we father, mother,
student, farm-hand,
senator or Head of State
—throughout the day—
we can feed the hungry
instruct the ignorant,
encourage the doubtful,
pray for the living and the dead.[84]

~

Anyone who wants to bring about unity
has only one right,
the right to serve everyone,
because in everyone
they serve God.[85]

Emptying ourselves
  —out of love for a neighbor—
  is deeply connected
  to the love that brings unity.[86]

~

We must be one
  with our neighbor
  not in an abstract way
  but in a real way (see Rm 12:15).
  Not in some future time but in the present.

One.
This means feeling within us
  what our neighbor feels,
  resolving our neighbor's problems
  as if they were our own,
  because they have been made our own
  by charity and for the love of Jesus
  in our neighbor (see Cor 9:19-22).[87]

The primary work
of the Work of Mary
is not the works of mercy,
but conversions.[88]

≈

People are truly loved by someone
if this someone is able to make them happy.
And so you can see why,
at times,
our love is not true love
when we become argumentative,
or show a certain attitude
or interest in things
that are of no interest
to our neighbor.[89]

We are called
in every moment
to lift up,
bring peace,
light,
especially joy,
to make the world smile.[90]

~

The behavior that best expresses
the word "love"
is: "making yourself one,"
going out to meet your neighbors
where they are, meeting their needs,
taking on what's burdening them,
helping them in their need,
taking on their pain.
Then, feeding the hungry,
giving drink to the thirsty,
offering advice, would have true meaning.[91]

By loving Jesus
in our neighbor,
we soon come to despise
the "old self" in us
and in our neighbor
(see Eph 4:22-24).[92]

~

It is Gospel-like
to feed the hungry and clothe the naked.
But taken on their own,
such actions might not express
the message of Jesus in all its beauty,
because such actions
could leave those on the receiving end
with a "beneficiary" complex.
Whereas the Gospel raises
every human being to the highest place,
as a son or a daughter
of God.[93]

When we are close to the sick
we should be like angels,
who go unnoticed
when they assist,
but whose absence is immediately felt.
This is love's way.[94]

~

Some are only called
to counsel
or instruct
or give shelter ...
We are called to give joy
—whether with or without these—
when making ourselves one with
our neighbors,
by feeding the hungry,
giving drink to the thirsty,
finding a job for someone,
visiting another,
being present to someone,
or simply helping out.[95]

It is natural that by loving
we are loved in return.
And a network of brotherhood
begins to grow among people
who were previously scattered,
indifferent to one another,
or even divided.[96]

~

Making ourselves one (see Cor 9:19-22)
and going against the current (see Lk 2:34),
are both love.
Because making ourselves one
is the attitude of love
and going against the current
is hatred for sin and love for God.
They are that work of love
—of direct or indirect mercy—
that can only be called
"admonishing sinners."[97]

Loving our neighbors
  has also led them
  to live the new commandment
  in their own way.[98]

∼

Mary went to her cousin Elizabeth
  in spite of the distance that separated them.
  The Work of Mary
  offers itself
  so that it might become
  a means of encounter
  between Jesus
  and his present-day precursors,
  so to speak; that is, between
  Jesus in Christians and those "seeds of the
  Word"
  which are present in the believers
  of other religions.[99]

$\mathcal{L}$ove.
  Does it just mean being good,
  merciful, patient, forgiving?
  No, not only.
  Jesus has shown us what love means.
  It means dying for our neighbor
  (see Jn 13:34-35; 15:13).

  Notice: "dying."
  Not: "being ready to die."
  We must die, denying ourselves
  by living our neighbor (see Mk 8:34).

  Again, love doesn't mean
  being prepared to die, love means dying
  for our neighbor.[100]

On the first Sorrowful Mystery
of the Rosary,
I remember that one day
I will be told of my death.
For now, I can prepare myself,
for that moment
by dying to myself
in every moment,
in my neighbor.[101]

⁓

After having loved
Jesus in our neighbor
all the day long, in the evening,
when we go to pray,
we often find ourselves
immersed in sweet union with God.[102]

$\mathcal{A}$ s far as we know
Mary never carried out any particular projects
for the sick or the poor ...
Yet she is rightfully called
"Health of the Sick,"
"Comfort of the Afflicted,"
"Refuge and Hope of Sinners."
Anyone who knows her
runs to her
because she is a Mother.[103]

~

" $\mathcal{T}$ oday
you will be with me
in Paradise" (Lk 23:43).

We should see each other
as God sees us,
not to criticize and condemn,
but to have mercy on,
and to help one another.[104]

$\mathcal{L}$ove and Truth.
Very often we falsify
the meaning of love
by considering it
only as a means
to the truth.
But love, too, is an absolute ...
for God is Love.[105]

~

$\mathcal{W}$e should revive our faith
by living Christian love
which pulverizes envy,
jealousy, criticism, judgment
and the other evils that can
make a hell out of
the precious gift
of life.[106]

Jesus identifies himself
with those who are suffering.
In the words addressed to Saul
Jesus expresses this:
"Saul, Saul, why do you persecute me?
And he said: 'Who are you, Lord?'
And he said: 'I am Jesus,
whom you are persecuting' " (Acts 9:4-5).

If others
do not make themselves one with us
in truth,
let us make ourselves one with them
in love.

God willing, the time will come
when the bond that unites us to our neighbor
will be Jesus among us,
and he is the Truth.[107]

Love of neighbor
   comes from love of God;
   but love for God
   blossoms in our hearts
   because we love our neighbor.[108]

~

We can show by our actions
   that love of neighbor
   is not an unattainable ideal
   —provided that one desires
   to relive the life of Jesus today.[109]

~

One of the straightest
   roads to God
   is our neighbor.[110]

Jesus, at Holy Communion
you give the whole of yourself
to each and every one.
In this way you help to shatter the illusion
we often have
when we think we are serving you
by organizing great works,
while we fail to recognize you
in those we meet every moment
of the day,
as if these encounters
were in no way connected
to our life in communion with you.[111]

~

To be consecrated
in virginity
means, literally, to play the part of Mary,
the Mother of all,
and to do so concretely,
silently, supernaturally,
here on earth,
wherever one may be.[112]

People
who sit from morning to night
at a desk, managing and discussing
the great problems of the world,
often end by being unable to understand
the few problems that weigh
on those who live nearest to them.
And Jesus commanded us to love and serve
our fellow-man.[113]

The love
that's been poured into our hearts
is a sharing in God's
divine *agape* love.
This love is spontaneous,
always new
continually finding new ways
to express itself.
It can't be categorized,
and invents unforeseeable solutions.[114]

Today's poor:
the addicts, the alienated,
the unemployed, the sinners,
the amoral, the unbelievers.
Let us reach out to them
and relive what Jesus did.
In this way we live and work,
awaiting the day when Jesus
will say to us: "I was an outsider
and you brought me into your group,
I was on drugs and you gave me happiness,
I was unemployed and your found me a job,
I had no standards to live by,
and you showed me God's law,
I was without God,
and you made me rediscover him
as Love."[115]

Perfection
does not consist in ideas
or wisdom,
but in charity,
in love for others.[116]

~

"God's love
has been poured
into our hearts
through the Holy Spirit
which has been given
to us" (Rom 5:5).

We love Jesus in others,
but it is also Jesus in us
who loves.[117]

The presence of love in the world
is like the coming of the sun in springtime,
when the arid and miserly earth
seems to have nothing to offer,
but instead unexpectedly grows again
and blossoms. The seed was there,
but there was no warmth, no love.[118]

~

We should reach out
to the poor and suffering,
prisoners and sinners,
with a supernatural attitude.
A Christian should be able to say:
"I have not come for those who are well,
but for the sick. Not for the just,
but for sinners" (Mk 2:17).[119]

God
my neighbor
me.[120]

Our Lady's love,
a mother's love,
is so unique
because she loves her children
as herself,
actually seeing herself in them.
We can also find something of ourselves in
others.
We can find Jesus
our Brother
in them.[121]

Never forget
the invisible
but real and constant presence
of Mary
who watches over Jesus in you.
She watches him there
as when she watched over him in Nazareth,
where he grew in age, in wisdom and in
grace.[122]

~

Human beings
are not instruments
for loving God.
From the moment
that the Word became flesh,
became one with us (Gal 3:28),
we no longer seek him
in the far-off heavens,
but in each neighbor as well.[123]

God very quickly
made it clear to me
that loving him
involved loving him
in every neighbor
as well.[124]

~

Love,
which leads to reciprocity,
has the power to build
the Christian community.
"Love builds up" (Cor 8:1).
A Christian community is built
with love.[125]

Jesus asks
St. Catherine of Siena:
"Who are those who have love
for their neighbors?
They are another Me,
united to me in love
with the wedding garment
of love."
Love divinizes us,
makes us sharers in Jesus'
divinity.[126]

~

The heart
of Jesus' message
is love, always love.
This is why he doesn't want
Christians to condemn anyone.
Jesus wants mercy
for all.[127]

*L*ove
    is not mere benevolence,
    which reaches no further
    than the one it helps.
    Christian goodness
    passes on
    to God.[128]

                    ∼

*W*e cannot love
    halfway,
    or without putting our heart into it.
    Jesus wants a love
    that moves us to compassion (see Lk 10:33).[129]

"In this is love,
not that we loved God but that he loved us ..."
(1 Jn 14:10-11).

In loving
we should do as God does:
not wait to be loved,
but be the first to love.
And since we cannot
do this with God
because he is always the first to love,
we should put this into practice
with each of our neighbors.[130]

~

We must give ourselves
totally to our neighbor
and receive him or her
into our hearts (see Lk 10:33).[131]

$\mathcal{A}$ servant does only
what the Master commands.
If all people,
or even just a small group of people
were really servants of God
in their "neighbors"
the world would soon belong to Christ.[132]

~

$\mathcal{O}$ur greatest treasure are the poor.
They're Jesus:
"You did it to me" (Mt 25:40b).[133]

~

$\mathcal{L}$ike St. Paul:
though free
and belonging to no one,
may we make ourselves
the slaves of all
in order to win
as many as possible.[134]

$\mathcal{A}$ person
who wishes
to bring Unity
should keep himself
in such humility
that he is ready to give up
—in favor of God and neighbor—
even his very own soul.

And if he does enter into himself,
it is only to pray
for his brothers and sister
and for himself.
He should be "in love"
with the will of his neighbor
whom he wants to serve
for God.[135]

"Your eye is the lamp of your body.
So if your eye is healthy,
your whole body will be full of light.
But if your eye is unhealthy,
your whole body will be full of darkness.
And if the light in you is darkness,
how great will that darkness be!"
(Mt 6:22-23).

A simple eye = seeing one *only* Father.
Only one outlook = serving *only* God
in every neighbor;
having one *only* brother: Jesus.

A healthy eye
is able to discern
Christ in every neighbor.[136]

We place ourselves
  at the service of Jesus
  in everyone we meet,
  so that Jesus in them
  will grow
  in wisdom, and age and grace
  (see Lk 5:52).[137]

~

Open your sight
  and see that
  every neighbor,
  rich or poor,
  ugly or pretty,
  capable or not:
  it is Jesus
  who draws near.[138]

"Truly I tell you,
in so far as you did it
for one of the least of these,
you did it for me" (Mt 25:40).

What a deep impression
these words leave in our souls!
What a powerful urge to live them!
What goodness Jesus had
in revealing them to us![139]

~

All things
are to be treated
with the love of the
Father for the Son!
What deep love!
And what a smile
from God,
smiling through our eyes,
on all things![140]

$\mathcal{L}$ove means *giving yourself*:
thinking of your neighbor,
living your neighbor.
I am Jesus forsaken
by living Jesus Forsaken
in my neighbor.[141]

~

"$\mathcal{T}$he love of God
has been poured out
in our hearts" (Rm 5:3-8).

We should love
those who draw near to us
as God loves them,
each one of them,
one at a time.
The love
in our hearts
should be pure
and only Holy Spirit.[142]

We need to
expand our hearts
to the measure
of the *Heart of Jesus*.
What a task!
This is that one thing needful.
This is done,
all is done.[143]

~

Just as one Sacred Host,
from among all the Hosts on this earth,
is enough to nourish us
with God,
so too, one neighbor,
the one God places near to us,
is enough for us
to communicate with humanity,
which is the mystical Jesus
on earth.[144]

Grant me, my God,
to be the tangible sacrament
of your Love,
of your being Love,
your arms
that clasp to your heart
and consume in your love
all the loneliness
of this world.[145]

Notes

1. Leonor Maria Salierno, *Maria nel pensiero di Chiara Lubich* (Rome: Città Nuova, 1993), p. 65.

2. Ibid., p. 46.

3. Chiara Lubich, *Yes, Yes, No, No* (London: New City, 1977), p. 8.

4. Chiara Lubich, *L'amore del prossimo* (Rome: Città Nuova, 2012), p. 18.

5. Chiara Lubich, *When Did We See You, Lord?* (New York: New City Press, 1979), p. 11.

6. Lubich, *Yes, Yes, No, No*, p. 58

7. Lubich, *When Did We See You, Lord?*, p. 12.

8. Salierno, *Maria nel pensiero di Chiara Lubich*, p. 72.

9. Lubich, *When Did We See You, Lord?*, p. 12.

10. Salierno, *Maria nel pensiero di Chiara Lubich*, p. 83.

11. Lubich, *Yes, Yes, No, No*, p. 22.

12. Lubich, *When Did We See You, Lord?*, p. 12.

13. Ibid.

14. Lubich, *Yes, Yes, No, No*, p. 22.

15. Salierno, *Maria nel pensiero di Chiara Lubich*, p. 24.

16. Ibid., p. 166.

17. Ibid., p. 167.

18. Lubich, *Yes, Yes, No, No*, p. 58

19. Ibid.

20. Lubich, *When Did We See You, Lord?*, p. 12.

21. Lubich, *Yes, Yes, No, No*, p. 68.

22. Lubich, *When Did We See You, Lord?*, p. 12.

23. Lubich, *Yes, Yes, No, No*, p. 127.

24. Ibid., p. 80.

25. Ibid.

26. Lubich, *When Did We See You, Lord?*, p. 13.

27. Lubich, *Yes, Yes, No, No*, p. 105.

28. Ibid., p. 108.

29. Michele Vandeleene, *Io, il Fratello, Dio nel pensiero di Chiara Lubich* (Rome: Città Nuova, 1993), p. 173.

30. Lubich, *Yes, Yes, No, No*, p. 110.

31. Lubich, *When Did We See You, Lord?*, p. 19.

32. Lubich, *Yes, Yes, No, No*, p. 115.

33. Ibid., p. 122.

34. Lubich, *Yes, Yes, No, No*, p. 127.

35. Salierno, *Maria nel pensiero di Chiara Lubich*, p. 169.

36. Ibid.

37. Salierno, *Maria nel pensiero di Chiara Lubich*, p. 65.

38. Ibid.

39. Ibid., p. 176.

40. Lubich, *Yes, Yes, No, No*, p. 130.

41. Salierno, *Maria nel pensiero di Chiara Lubich*, p. 168.

42. Chiara Lubich, *Stirrings of Unity* (New York: New City Press, 1964), p. 86.

43. Salierno, *Maria nel pensiero di Chiara Lubich*, p. 87.

44. Ibid., p. 125.

45. Ibid., p. 96.

46. Lubich, *When Did We See You, Lord?*, p. 13.

47. Salierno, *Maria nel pensiero di Chiara Lubich*, p. 111.

48. Ibid., p. 169.

49. Ibid., p. 21.

50. Ibid., p. 170.

51. Ibid., p. 167.

52. Ibid.

53. Ibid., p. 168.

54. Ibid.

55. Ibid., p. 170.

56. Ibid.

57. Ibid.

58. Ibid., p. 173.

59. Ibid.

60. Ibid.

61. Lubich, *When Did We See You, Lord?*, p. 13.

62. Salierno, *Maria nel pensiero di Chiara Lubich*, p. 173.

63. Ibid., p. 174.

64. Lubich, *When Did We See You, Lord?*, p. 35.

65. Salierno, *Maria nel pensiero di Chiara Lubich*, p. 173.

66. Vandeleene, *Io, il Fratello, Dio nel pensiero di Chiara Lubich*, p. 173.

67. Ibid.

68. Ibid.

69. Ibid.

70. Ibid., p. 175.

71. Ibid.

72. Ibid., p. 125.

73. Salierno, *Maria nel pensiero di Chiara Lubich*, p. 125.

74. Ibid.

75. Vandeleene, *Io, il Fratello, Dio nel pensiero di Chiara Lubich*, p. 175.

76. Ibid.

77. Lubich, *When Did We See You, Lord?*, p. 105.

78. Vandeleene, *Io, il Fratello, Dio nel pensiero di Chiara Lubich*, p. 175.

79. Ibid., p. 176.

80. Ibid.

81. Ibid., p. 177.

82. Ibid.

83. Lubich, *When Did We See You, Lord?*, p. 14.

84. Vandeleene, *Io, il Fratello, Dio nel pensiero di Chiara Lubich*, p. 175.

85. Ibid.

86. Ibid., p. 179.

87. Ibid., p. 177.

88. Ibid., p. 182.

89. Ibid., p. 178.

90. Ibid.

91. Ibid.

92. Ibid., p. 183.

93. Ibid., p. 179.

94. Lubich, *Stirrings of Unity*, p. 83.

95. Vandeleene, *Io, il Fratello, Dio nel pensiero di Chiara Lubich*, p. 179.

96. Ibid., p. 184.

97. Ibid.

98. Ibid., p. 183.

99. Lubich, *When Did We See You, Lord?*, p. 16.

100. Vandeleene, *Io, il Fratello, Dio nel pensiero di Chiara Lubich*, p. 189.

101. Salierno, *Maria nel pensiero di Chiara Lubich*, p. 157.

102. Lubich, *When Did We See You, Lord?*, p. 105.

103. Salierno, *Maria nel pensiero di Chiara Lubich*, p. 144.

104. Chiara Lubich, *Stirrings of Unity*, p. 80.

105. Ibid., p. 83.

106. Ibid.

107. Ibid., p. 41.

108. Lubich, *When Did We See You, Lord?*, p. 104.

109. Ibid., p. 14.

110. Lubich, *Stirrings of Unity*, p. 82.

111. Ibid., p. 81.

112. Ibid., p. 86.

113. Ibid., p. 52.

114. Lubich, *When Did We See You, Lord?*, p. 110.

115. Ibid., p. 68.

116. Lubich, *Stirrings of Unity*, p. 81.

117. Lubich, *When Did We See You, Lord?*, p. 110.

118. Lubich, *Stirrings of Unity*, p. 82.

119. Vandeleene, *Io, il Fratello, Dio nel pensiero di Chiara Lubich*, p. 54.

120. Lubich, *When Did We See You, Lord?*, p. 103.

121. Salierno, *Maria nel pensiero di Chiara Lubich*, p. 160.

122. Ibid., p. 145.

123. Lubich, *When Did We See You, Lord?*, p. 115.

124. Ibid., p. 102.

125. Salierno, *Maria nel pensiero di Chiara Lubich*, p. 114.

126. Lubich, *When Did We See You, Lord?*, p. 116.

127. Salierno, *Maria nel pensiero di Chiara Lubich*, p. 147.

128. Lubich, *When Did We See You, Lord?*, p. 114.

129. Ibid., p. 114.

130. Ibid., p. 110.

131. Lubich, *When Did We See You, Lord?*, p. 115.

132. Michele Vandeleene (ed.), *Chiara Lubich, La dottrina spirituale* (Rome: Città Nuova, 2009), p. 56.

133. Chiara Lubich, *L'amore del prossimo*, (Rome: Citta Nuova, 2012) p.14-15.

134. Michele Vandeleene (ed.), *Chiara Lubich, La dottrina spirituale* (Rome: Città Nuova, 2009), p. 55.

135. Ibid.

136. Ibid.

137. Ibid.

138. Chiara Lubich, in *Città Nuova Magazine* (1958), No. 15-16, 5-20, p. 3.

139. Chiara Lubich, *L'amore del prossimo*, p. 14.

140. Ibid., p. 16.

141. Ibid., p. 20.

142. Ibid., p. 19.

143. Ibid., p. 18.

144. Ibid.

145. Ibid., p. 20.

For Further Reading

Chiara Lubich, *Essential Writings: Spirituality, Dialogue, Culture* (Hyde Park, NY: New City Press, 2007).

Thomas Masters and Amy Uelman, *Focolare, Living a Spirituality of Unity in the United States* (Hyde Park, NY: New City Press, 2011).

Chiara Lubich, A New Way: *The Spirituality of Unity* (Hyde Park, NY: New City Press, 2006).

Chiara Lubich, *The Art of Loving* (Hyde Park, NY: New City Press, 2010).

Periodicals

Living City Magazine, www.livingcity-magazine.org

On line Resources

http://www.centrochiaralubich.org/en/documents/texts.html   - this site enables you to search some of the writings of Chiara Lubich.